USING A NET

by Jessica Quilty

Scott Foresman
is an imprint of

Glenview, Illinois • Boston, Massachusetts • Chandler, Arizona
Upper Saddle River, New Jersey

Every effort has been made to secure permission and provide appropriate credit for photographic material. The publisher deeply regrets any omission and pledges to correct errors called to its attention in subsequent editions.

Unless otherwise acknowledged, all photographs are the property of Scott Foresman, a division of Pearson Education.

Photo locators denoted as follows: Top (T), Center (C), Bottom (B), Left (L), Right (R), Background (Bkgd)

Opener: ©Michael S. Yamashita/CORBIS; 1 ©Anthony Bannister; Gallo Images/CORBIS; 3 ©Michael Freeman/CORBIS; 4 ©Michael S. Yamashita/CORBIS; 6 ©Julie Habel/CORBIS; 7 ©Anthony Bannister; Gallo Images/CORBIS; 8 ©Phil Schermeister/CORBIS

ISBN 13: 978-0-328-50837-2
ISBN 10:   0-328-50837-3

5 6 7 8 9 10   V010 15 14 13 12

These fishermen caught many fish today!

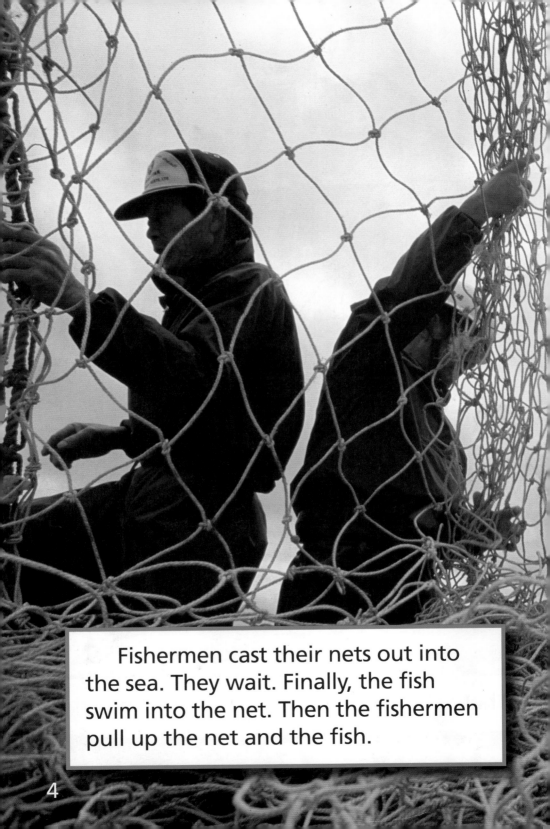

Fishermen cast their nets out into the sea. They wait. Finally, the fish swim into the net. Then the fishermen pull up the net and the fish.

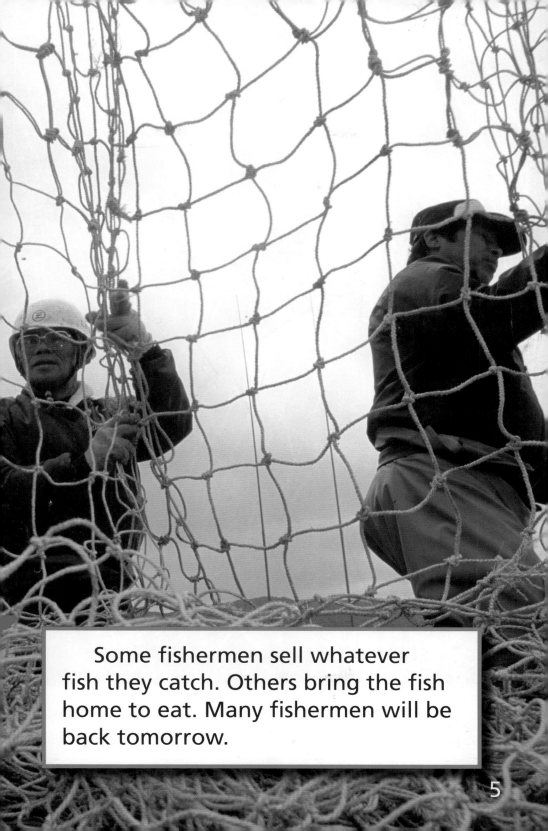

Some fishermen sell whatever fish they catch. Others bring the fish home to eat. Many fishermen will be back tomorrow.

Think about this: How are a fishing net and a web like this one the same?

The spider spins a web with silk thread. Can you believe one little spider can build something like this?

The spider is hungry after all its work. The spider will eat whatever has been caught in the net.